FIRST GUIDE TO
DRAGONFLIES
OF SOUTHERN AFRICA

Small Scarlet (page 41)

Lakeside Dropwing (page 48)

WARREN & VIENESSA GOODWIN

Contents

Black-pointed Skimmer (page 35)

Struik Publishers
(a division of New Holland Publishing
(South Africa) (Pty) Ltd)
80 McKenzie Street,
Cape Town, 8001 South Africa

New Holland Publishing is a member
of Johnnic Communications Ltd.
Visit us at www.struik.co.za
Log on to our photographic website
www.imagesofafrica.co.za
for an African experience.

Copyright © text:
Warren & Vienessa Goodwin, 2003
Copyright © photographs: individual
photographers as credited on page 57, 2003
Copyright © maps:
Warren & Vienessa Goodwin, 2003
Copyright © published edition:
Struik Publishers, 2003

First published in 2003

1 3 5 7 9 10 8 6 4 2

Editor: Emily Bowles
Designer: Heston Michaels

Reproduction Hirt & Carter
Cape (Pty) Ltd

Printed and bound by Paarl Print

ISBN: 1 86872 850 1

Introduction

The purpose of this book is to introduce some of the more common and easily identifiable species of dragonflies that may be encountered in southern Africa. It is not intended as a comprehensive guide, but we hope that it will stimulate an interest in these fascinating insects.

There are about 5 000 dragonfly species worldwide – of which around 210 species are known to occur in southern and central Africa. The best places to find dragonflies are areas within, or bordering on, wetlands.

Dragonflies belong to the order of insects called Odonata. Most people are familiar with the dragonfly as a brightly coloured insect with a long, slender body and two pairs of transparent wings. Although they are known collectively as dragonflies, these insects actually belong to two main suborders: damselflies or Zygoptera, which have even fore- and hindwings, and dragonflies or Anisoptera, which have uneven fore- and hindwings.

Types of Dragonfly

Damselflies, or **Zygopteran dragonflies**, are mostly small, brightly coloured and dainty insects. They occur in grasses, marshy areas, or riverine vegetation, where they spend a great deal of time perched in the shade with their wings folded, or partly folded, above the abdomen, flying periodically to catch small prey such as midges. Their flight appears weak and slow. They are the most abundant Odonata.

Damselflies are particularly difficult to identify because they vary greatly in size and markings, even among members and sexes of the same species. In addition, superficial similarities to unrelated species may occur in some cases. The only certain method of identification is to examine them under a microscope. Each species has a specific adaptation to mating that prevents crossbreeding between closely related species, so examination of genitalia and anal appendages[G] is crucial.

Glistening Demoiselle damselfly (page 23)

Some species of damselfly may be confused with the anatomically similar lacewings (antlions), belonging to the order Neuroptera. However, lacewings have longer antennae, and are purely terrestrialG. Unlike dragonflies, lacewings are nocturnalG in the adult stage, and are often attracted to lights at night.

Anisopteran dragonflies are specially adapted to their highly active, carnivorous, and mostly diurnalG lifestyle. These are the more active dragonflies that spend a great deal of the day hunting in flight and are thus most often built robustly. Males of most Anisopteran species are highly territorial and colourful, defending their area by patrolling and perching conspicuously. Any intruding male is attacked, often resulting in damaged wings

Females can be difficult to identify unless caught along with the male while mating. Larger species, such as *Anax* species (see pages 27–9) and *Pantala flavescens* (see page 53) can be identified by sight. The blue *Orthetrum* species are among the most difficult to identify. Again, the only way to be certain of identification is to examine the genitalia under a microscope.

Blue Emperor dragonfly (page 28)

Anatomy

Dragonflies (Odonata) range in length from 20 to 80 mm. Like all insects, their bodies are divided into three different sections: the head; the thorax or middle division (the front part of which is the prothorax); and the abdomen, which is comparatively long and narrow in shape.

Head: Dragonflies have a pair of distinctive compound eyes that contain up to 30 000 facets each, as well as three simple eyes that detect light and movement, but not shape or form. They require excellent eyesight in order to capture fast-moving and cryptically marked prey. The compound eyes of damselflies (Zygoptera) are, without exception, separated by the occiput, or upper section of the head behind the eyes, while those of dragonflies (Anisoptera) generally meet across the occiput. (The large group of primitive dragonflies known as Gomphids is the only exception here.) Both dragonfly suborders have unique compound jaws, which are arranged in such a way that they slice and shred a food item from all sides. Prey is thus quickly and efficiently consumed, even on the wing.

Thorax: The three pairs of legs are positioned far forward on the thorax and prothorax to enable dragonflies to perch efficiently and to catch their prey, which consists of smaller insects and, in some of the larger species, even other dragonflies. The legs of a dragonfly are armed with a pair of claws or barbs on the lower segments, which hook and hold prey securely for eating. Breathing occurs via pores called *thoracic spiracles* that are situated along the sides of the thorax.

Abdomen: All dragonflies have ten segments on the abdomen, numbered from the thorax outwards. A useful way of determining the sex of a dragonfly is to look for any appendages under the second abdominal segment. A male has genitalia here. He also has a pair of anal appendages[G] on the tenth segment of his abdomen, which he uses to clasp the female behind her head or thorax while mating. In contrast, the female has no appendages on her second abdominal segment and the tenth segment ends in a single pair of *stylets* or *cerci*[G], which are of little apparent use.

Wings: Speed and manoeuvrability are essential to an airborne predator. Dragonflies (Odonata) have two pairs of wings on the thorax, which are supported and reinforced by a complex arrangement of veins and strengthening features. This allows some large species to fly as fast as 60 km/h.

The structure of veins in the wings is a complex subject, but it is worth mentioning a few key wing characteristics, since these are often a critical tool used by

FIGURES 1 & 2: THE STRUCTURAL FEATURES OF A DRAGONFLY

1. labium (lower lip)
2. labrum (upper lip)
3. epistome (lower face)
4. frons (lower forehead)
5. vertex (upper forehead)
6. antenna
7. occiput (upper forehead, between or behind the compound eyes)
8. compound eye
9. prothorax
10. synthorax[G]
11. forewing
12. antenodal cross veins[G]
13. nodus
14. pterostigma (wing spot)
15. membranule (basal area)
16. hindwing
17. anal appendage
18. abdominal segments
19. accessory genitalia
20. thoracic spiracle (breathing pore)
21. femur
22. tibia (lower leg)
23. tarsus

DRAGONFLY WING MARGINS

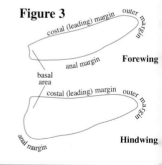

Figure 3

costal (leading) margin — outer margin

anal margin

basal area

Forewing

costal (leading) margin — outer margin

anal margin

Hindwing

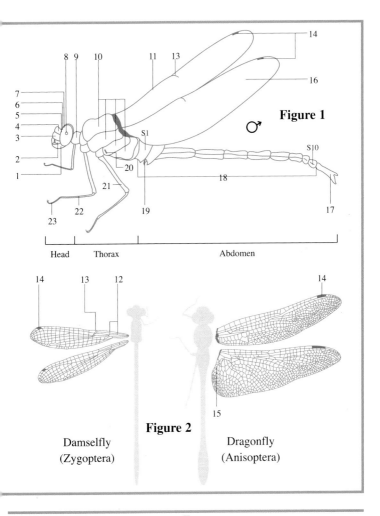

Figure 1

♂

Head   Thorax   Abdomen

Figure 2

Damselfly
(Zygoptera)

Dragonfly
(Anisoptera)

scientists to distinguish different species. The strengthening features include a notch (or *nodus*) on the leading edge of the wing and a thickened spot near the apex of the wing, which is known as the wing spot or *pterostigma*. This area is roughly rectangular and is usually a different colour to the rest of the wing (see page 7). The Glistening Demoiselle is the only exception, as it does not require this feature in the wing because its habits and preference for a well-wooded or forested habitat, do not require it to be a strong flier. The base of dragonfly wings is often supported on the anal margin by a *membranule*, which is a thickened vein in the basal area, i.e. that portion joining the wing to the thorax.

Dragonflies have far sturdier wings than damselflies. Unlike damselflies, dragonflies settle with their wings in the 'outstretched' position (like the wings of an aeroplane).

Life cycle

During mating, the male dragonfly holds the female's head or thorax with specially adapted anal appendages[G]. The female bends her abdomen backwards and upwards to hook into the male genitals, under the second segment of his abdomen, forming a characteristic shape that is often referred to as the 'tandem wheel' (see opposite). The larger Anisopteran dragonfly species almost always mate in flight, while damselflies often settle on vegetation. Dragonflies (Odonata) begin their lives in water. Certain female damselflies lay their eggs in holes that they have pierced in reeds. Most dragonflies lay their eggs randomly on, or below the surface of the water by dipping the abdomen below the surface, often in flight. The eggs are deposited by means of a specialized egg-laying organ called an *ovipositor* and are released in their hundreds. They resemble a mass of cooked sago pudding. In some migratory[G] species (such

The nymph^G of the Red Emperor (*Anax speratus*) is large in comparison with those of other species

years, depending on the species. During this period, the nymphs^G, which do not resemble the adults, feed voraciously on aquatic insect prey, and larger species may even feed on small fish and tadpoles. A nymph^G moves about actively, catching prey with its prehensile^G lower jaw, which acts as a 'spring-loaded' trap. Damselfly nymphs^G use a wriggling or swimming motion, while dragonfly nymphs^G use jet propulsion, made possible by forcing water through the breathing apparatus. The nymph^G develops comparatively slowly and sheds its skin a number of times. It leaves the

as the common Wandering Glider, see page 53), they are laid rapidly in shallow, temporary puddles. Masses of migratory^G dragonflies such as these often follow rain fronts for this purpose. They are very successful due to their sheer numbers and a comparatively shorter larval^G development period, which enables them to capitalize on the availability of water – where it is normally absent for most of the year.

The *larval* or *nymph*^G stage varies among dragonflies, lasting for as little as a month, or as long as three

March Bluetail male and female mating

empty husk of the body on or above the water, often on reeds or other vegetation from which it emerges as a soft-bodied *teneral*, or young adult dragonfly. At the teneral stage, the dragonfly is most vulnerable to predation, as it has a soft body and wings that take some hours to dry out, harden and colour. The wings are particularly iridescent at this stage. Dragonfly nymphsG often fall prey to fish, while those in the immature or full adult stages may become a meal for bigger predators such as bee-eaters.

Distribution

For the purposes of this book, southern Africa has been defined as incorporating all countries south of the Zambezi, Kunene and Okavango rivers. These include Botswana, Lesotho, most of Mozambique, Namibia, South Africa, Swaziland and Zimbabwe. These countries encompass nine habitat types. Note that all dragonflies are associated with seasonal or permanent water for

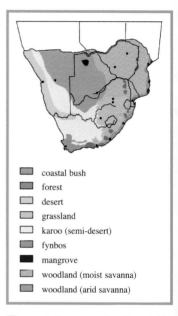

coastal bush
forest
desert
grassland
karoo (semi-desert)
fynbos
mangrove
woodland (moist savanna)
woodland (arid savanna)

The vegetation zones of southern Africa

breeding and feeding. At least six of the common, larger species of dragonfly in the region are migratoryG. Depending on the species, distances travelled can vary from a few to hundreds of kilometres. Common migrants, such as the Wandering Glider, (see page 53), for example, can be found in almost any habitat during the summer months, depending on food supply and rainfall.

The Okavango Delta in northern Botswana is renowned for its diversity of dragonflies, which is ascribed to the varied habitat of thick bush, forest patches and waterways lined with papyrus and phragmites plants. This provides diverse conditions favoured by resident and migratory[G] dragonflies for feeding, resting or breeding. Owing to this diverse environment, isolated in an otherwise dry area, seven species occur here that are found nowhere else.

Although southern Africa has an abundant dragonfly population, Zambia and other countries to the north have a higher diversity of species, possibly because of wetter conditions. Dragonflies and damselflies have adapted well to the artificial conditions created by gardens and swimming pools, and the ranges of some species have undoubtedly been extended by these newly created environments.

Collecting dragonflies

Collecting dragonflies for research or identification purposes is relatively easy and inexpensive. Initially, all that is required is a suitable entomologist's[G] net. The frame can be made by attaching a loop of fencing wire to a suitable wooden or aluminium handle by means of hose clamps. A ready-made fishing net can be adapted by replacing the nylon mesh with a generous amount of soft organza, which can easily be sewn. The diameter of the net should be 40–50 cm.

Damselflies are easily caught by 'sweeping' the net through grass or undergrowth, as they fly slowly. The faster, more alert species are difficult to catch, requiring more practice. Most species can be caught by simply waiting for the insect to alight on the ground or on a favourite perch. Once caught, dragonflies should be carefully removed from the net. Take care not to damage the wings or body. The dragonfly

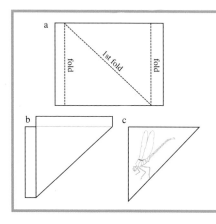

A SPECIMEN HOLDER

(a) This is easily made from a rectangle of paper about 150 mm by 100 mm.
(b) Fold the paper diagonally to leave equal tabs. Bend the tabs over.
(c) Open to insert the specimen, re-fold and label a tab for identification.

can then be killed by carefully squeezing the sides of the thorax between thumb and forefinger. This forces the wings into an upward position and exposes the genitalia, which later facilitates identification and storage. If you simply want to examine a live specimen, then hold it by the wings, again between the thumb and forefinger, before releasing it. Collectors should never be tempted to collect more specimens from one area than absolutely necessary, as this may cause some disturbance to these populations.

Specimens can be placed in triangular paper or cellophane envelopes on which the date, name of collector, locality and any other relevant details are recorded for future reference. It is good practice to note the

Black-pointed Skimmer (page 35)

Rock Dropwing (page 49)

markings of the live specimen as some lose their colour after death. Wing shape and markings should all be noted for identification. Specimens should be stored in a suitable box with naphthalene^G in order to prevent damage by insects such as ants.

Once identified, collected dragonflies that have been dried in the 'closed' wing position can be pinned to a board. This can be achieved by 'softening' the specimen in a 'relaxing box' (a plastic lunchbox with a tight-fitting lid is ideal for this purpose). A layer of plaster of Paris or cotton wool should be placed at the bottom of the box and moistened with a few drops of water and disinfectant, which prevents mould from growing. The specimen can then be placed on a plate or similar receptacle on top of this layer and the lid of the box tightly closed. Twelve hours should be sufficient for the 'softening' process to be completed, after which the specimen can be manipulated to the required form.

Bear in mind, though, that dragonflies are beautiful creatures, best left in their natural environment, where they are interesting and rewarding to observe.

Myths

Many people mistakenly believe that dragonflies are dangerous: they are known as 'horse stingers', 'devils' darning needles' and, in Afrikaans, as 'naaldekokers' (needle cases or quivers). In fact, dragonflies are harmless to humans and have no sting. Along with other carnivorous insects, they actually help to control the populations of smaller insects and thus play an important role in the ecosystem.

How to use this book

All species included in this book are common and thus likely to be encountered in the field. Each species account contains information under the following headings:

Species name: Only recently have African species been given common names, and these form the main heading for each species. Scientific names appear in italics below the common name. These are binomial, i.e. 'double-barrelled'. The first part (or generic name) is shared by closely related species, while the second is the specific or species name. Some subspecies (or races) are included in this book. These groups are most often geographically separated and show slight variations, but the differences are not significant enough for the group to be classed as a separate species. Subspecies are given trinomial or 'triple-barrelled' names. Note that the original species described is called the nominate race.

Average size: This section refers to total body length. Some abdominal lengths are provided in the species descriptions, as this may assist when identifying a specimen in the 'wings-folded position'. Wingspan is normally not used to identify specimens as this is not considered a distinguishing feature in most dragonflies. Hindwing lengths are considered important in some *Orthetrum* species and, where

Pied-spot immature male (page 38)

relevant, these have been provided in the text.

Description: Descriptions are included in order to complement the photographs provided and to assist in identification. The pterostigma or wing spot can be a diagnostic feature in some species. Females and young adults are often quite different in colouring from the adult males, which, generally, are more brightly marked. Only where there is a significant distinguishing feature in the female of a species is it noted in the text. Identifying dragonflies and damselflies can be difficult, often requiring quite complex scientific terms and a microscope. The descriptions provided here are simplified for ease of use; however, the correct scientific terms are given in the illustrations on pages 6–7.

Habitat and habits: 'Habitat' discusses the preferred vegetation type of each species in association with a specific type of wetland (where relevant). The behaviour or traits that may assist in singling out a particular species or group among others is described under 'habits'.

Distribution: As a rule, dragonflies do not occur in true deserts or far from water (with the exception of migratoryG dragonflies). Distribution is explained under this heading and is accompanied by maps showing approximate dispersal. Where relevant, distributions outside of the southern African region are described for the reader's interest.

Wheeling Glider (page 54)

Pale Spreadwing

Lestes pallidus

Average size: ± 58 mm.

Description: Very varied in appearance, ranging in colour from yellowish to light brown. Settles with semi-open wings. The striking wing spot is typically yellow and black and is quite conspicuous (± 1,5 mm long). The abdomen is unusually long and slender (± 32 mm), both sexes being generally similar in size and colour. At least 6 forms of this damselfly occur in southern Africa.

Habitat and habits: Occurs in open, grassy country but is absent from forests. Found near reedy pools and streams, and in bush near water. Feeds on small flying insects such as midges.

Distribution: Common in southern Africa, and encountered throughout Africa. Found in suitable habitat from the Western Cape eastwards and northwards, in Zimbabwe and Mozambique, and to the west in northern Botswana and northern Namibia. Abundant in the Okavango Delta.

Common Pond Damsel

Ceriagrion glabrum

Average size:
± 42 mm.

Description: The synthorax[G] of this damselfly ranges from vivid orange to red, or brown and green in individuals, sometimes being totally green in females. The eyes are generally green. Pond Damsels are readily distinguished by their bright red and orange lower face and abdomen. In males, the anal appendage (segment 10) has prominent posterior[G] teeth, which it uses to hold the female during copulation. Females are generally duller in colour than males.

Habitat and habits: Occurs in open country, woodland, dense bush or in light forest near pools, swamps, streams and rivers. Feeds on small flying insects.

Distribution: Common in suitable habitat in most parts of southern Africa, except in the very dry areas to the west. Widespread on the African continent. Also occurs in parts of the Middle East.

Painted Sprite

Pseudagrion hageni tropicanum

Average size:
± 33 mm.

Description: Best distinguished by the orange upper lip and eyes. Each wing has a rust-coloured wing spot. The lower face has a broad orange frontal stripe, while a diagonal green stripe runs along the black chest region. The abdomen is dark dorsally[G] and pale below. Towards the rear of the abdomen there are unmistakable alternating black and blue dorsal[G] bands (on segments 7–9). A blue ventral[G] spot distinguishes the anal appendage[G]. Female Painted Sprite damselflies are duller in colour than males.

Habitat and habits: Occurs near bush, woodland, forest and well-shaded streams. May occur in large numbers.

Distribution: This subspecies is common in South Africa – from the Eastern Cape to coastal KwaZulu-Natal and further north. Also found in Botswana, Namibia, most of Zimbabwe and Mozambique. A widespread damselfly, found as far north as equatorial east and west Africa.

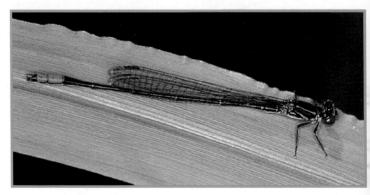

Kersten's Sprite

Pseudagrion kersteni

Average size:
± 34 mm.

Distribution: One of the most common damselflies. Found in suitable habitat from the Western Cape eastwards and northwards to Mozambique and Zimbabwe. Also found across northern Botswana and Namibia. This is an abundant species in most of Africa.

Description: Easily recognized by the black or dark brown lower lip. Compared with other damselflies the wing spot is not very elongated. The thorax is unmistakable, because of the pale diagonal stripe and the upper anal appendage[G], which protrudes noticeably from its lower section. Females are duller in colour than males.

Habitat and habits: Occurs near streams, rivers and pools. This species is absent from forests, swamps and extremely dry areas.

Riffle Sprite

Pseudagrion sublacteum

Average size:
± 40 mm.

Description: A fairly large damselfly with red eyes and upper forehead. The lower face is black at the base and the lower lip may be greenish-blue. The upper section of the synthorax^G is normally red, or occasionally yellow, and there are thick black divisions between the other thoracic segments. The abdomen may have dark markings above and between the abdominal segments. Another distinguishing feature is the unbranched upper anal appendage^G, which is longer than the lower anal appendage^G. Abdominal segments 8, 9, and 10 are bluish in colour. The wing spot is reddish. Sexes are similar; however, mature males may develop a powdery purple coating over the body and, sometimes, a pale blue thorax.

Habitat and habits: Found at grassy streams or rivers with flowing waters but also favours swamps with some water current.

Distribution: Found in suitable habitat from KwaZulu-Natal northwards to Mozambique, Zimbabwe, Botswana and northern Namibia. Also occurs from Zambia to east and west Africa. This species was originally described from Togo.

March Bluetail

Ischnura senegalensis

Average size: ± 32 mm.

Description: A variable species. The thorax and abdomen of females are dull orange up to the second segment, with a black-edged stripe at the top of the synthorax[G] and along the top of the abdomen. The face is largely black above. The base of the abdomen may be greenish-blue or dull yellow. Males differ in that they are blue from the thorax up to the second segment of the abdomen. The synthorax[G] is black above, while segments 7–10 of the abdomen form a black swelling with a blue band near segment 8 and at the base of segments 9 and 10. The top half of each eye is black, containing a tiny blue dot. The wing spot often differs in colour between the fore- and hindwings.

Habitat and habits: Occurs under diverse conditions, except in very arid regions or in dense forest. Tolerant of highly saline waters. The most abundant damselfly in Africa.

Distribution: Common in southern Africa. Found in all suitable habitats from the Western Cape eastwards and northwards through South Africa, Mozambique, and Zimbabwe, and across northern Botswana into Namibia. Occurs throughout most of Africa. Also found in Asia and in the Philippines.

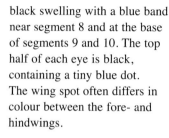

Swamp Bluet

Africallagma glaucum

Average size: ± 21–23 mm.

Description: A small damselfly with a solid black wing spot on each wing. Easily distinguished by the vivid blue thorax, which bears two black diagonal stripes. The upper segments of each leg have black markings along their upper sides. Other distinguishing features are the blue eyes and lower forehead as well as the mouth regions and front part of the thorax, which are black. The upper part of the anal appendage[G] (on the tenth segment of the thorax) is markedly short. Females have a dull appearance, and may be larger than males.

Habitat and habits: Occurs in bush, woodland or riverine shade. Absent from open, arid regions and dense forest. Feeds on small flying insects such as midges.

Distribution: Common in southern Africa. Encountered in all suitable habitats from the Western Cape eastwards and northwards through South Africa, Mozambique, Zimbabwe and across northern Botswana into Namibia. Occurs over most of Africa.

Glistening Demoiselle

Phaon iridipennis

Average size:
± 66 mm.

Description: This is a large damselfly that is dull brownish-green in colour, and may have green diagonal stripes on the synthorax[G]. The abdomen is particularly long and there are no wing spots on the iridescent wings. The sexes are generally alike.

Habitat and habits: Occurs in woodland, bush, swamps and lakes. Not found in very arid regions. Feeds on small insects such as midges.

Distribution: A common species in southern Africa. It is found in all suitable habitats from the Western Cape, through most of South Africa, eastwards and northwards to Mozambique and Zimbabwe, and across northern Botswana into Namibia. Encountered as far north as Somalia and westwards to Senegal. There is also a race in Madagascar.

Dancing Jewel

Platycypha caligata

Average size:
± 30 mm.

Description: This beautiful species belongs to a subfamily that typically has a shorter, broader abdomen than other damselflies. In males, the sides of the thorax tend to be red in colour. The sides of abdominal segments 1–3 are distinctly red. Segment 1 is black, with red lateral[G] patches, while the second is black above, with blue spots in the centre and at each end. The lower legs of adult males are white on the inner sides, while those of immature males are yellow. The male's brightly coloured legs are used in an elaborate courtship display from which this species derives its common name. The female is comparatively non-descript, being a dull grey.

Habitat and habits: This damselfly occurs near running streams or rivers, in bush or forest on river banks, in rocky areas or sometimes on sand-banks. It is not found in swamps.

Distribution: A fairly common species that generally occurs in hilly or mountainous areas in KwaZulu-Natal, Botswana, Zimbabwe, Mozambique and in areas bordering the Okavango Delta. Also encountered in Ethiopia, Somalia, and Guinea-Bissau.

Common Tigertail

Ictinogomphus ferox

Average size:
± 75 mm.

Description: This large dragon-fly species has protruding eyes that do not meet in the centre of the upper forehead. It has a heavy thorax and a long, thin abdomen (± 50 mm), which tapers outwards at the eighth abdominal segment to a modified ninth and tenth segment. The greenish-yellow thorax has black or brown stripes, while alternating black and yellow segments mark the abdomen. The anal appendages[G] are yellow. This species has long wings, and the black wing spot is ± 8 mm long. The lower legs are black and yellow. Males and females are similar in appearance.

Habitat and habits: Occurs near reedy streams, rivers and pools or lakes. A fast flier, but often settles on reeds or the branches of trees.

Distribution: Common from the Northern Cape (Orange River) to KwaZulu-Natal, north to Mozambique and Zimbabwe, west to northern and eastern Botswana and into northern Namibia. Also extends into East Africa and across to Senegal.

Common Hooktail

Paragomphus genei

Average size:
± 44 mm.

Description: As with the Common Tigertail (see page 25), this dragonfly species has protruding eyes that do not meet in the centre of the upper forehead. The abdomen is yellow and brown and the thorax greenish. The eighth, ninth and tenth abdominal segments have appendages that gradually become smaller. These appendages are somewhat larger in the male. The wings are noticeably shorter than the abdomen. Females are similar to males in appearance, but have a slightly broader abdomen. In both sexes the yellow abdominal segments have alternating brown divisional lines and spots. The lower forehead and lower lip vary from yellow to green.

Habitat and habits: Occurs in bush country and in open or arid country near streams, rivers or pools. Absent from forests and extremely arid areas. It settles briefly on rocks, sand or branches.

Distribution: This dragonfly is widespread and common in southern Africa. It belongs to a large family of primitive dragonflies called the Gomphids, and is the most abundant member of this group found on the continent.

Vagrant Emperor

Anax ephippiger

Average size:
± 70 mm.

Description: This dragonfly species can be identified by the bright blue saddle on the upper part of the second abdominal segment. The wings are clear, with a yellow tinge, while the wing spot is orange-yellow and the abdomen is greenish-yellow and black. It is a large species – the abdomen is approximately 43 mm long. The sexes are similar in appearance.

Habitat and habits: Occurs in all habitat types, except for true deserts. It tends to hover and hawk^G over streams and pools in open bush country and is very alert and fast flying; it may fly to great heights to avoid danger. Diurnal^G but may be seen flying at dusk. A migratory^G species.

Distribution: A fairly common species, found during the summer months throughout southern Africa, with the possible exception of the Namib Desert. Occurs in most parts of Africa, as well as in southern Europe and western Asia.

Blue Emperor

Anax imperator mauricianus

Average size:
± 75 mm.

Description: A large, robust dragonfly, easily recognized by its brilliant green thorax and its bright blue abdomen (± 50 mm long) covered in black spots. The thorax is a duller green in the female. In the hand, another distinguishing feature is the dark spot on top of the yellow lower forehead.

Distribution: This species is common in southern Africa. Occurs in suitable habitat from the Western Cape eastwards and northwards through South Africa, Mozambique, Zimbabwe and right across northern Botswana into Namibia. Found throughout most of Africa in association with permanent water. *Anax imperator* is found in most of Europe and west Africa, while *A. i. mauricianus* is widespread over sub-Saharan Africa.

Habitat and habits: This wide-spread migrant[G] is found in most localities that are not heavily wooded, hawking[G] over pools, swamps, streams or rivers. This species is an extremely fast flier, and is very alert. Feeds on large insects and smaller dragonflies.

Orange Emperor

Anax speratus

Average size:
± 75 mm.

Description: A large orange to red dragonfly with an abdomen of between 50 and 54 mm in length. The wing spot is red and, unlike other 'red' *Anax* species, the forewing does not have brown, transparent markings at the base, although these may occur on the hindwing. Females and immature males may have a green thorax, but are otherwise similar to males.

Habitat and habits: Occurs in bush or woodland. This species is seen flying along streams and rivers searching for prey, which includes other dragonflies. It does not hover or hawkG like other *Anax* species, but is nevertheless an alert and fast-flying species.

Distribution: Fairly common in southern Africa. Found in suitable habitats from the Western Cape eastwards and northwards through South Africa, Mozambique and Zimbabwe and across northern Botswana into Namibia. Occurs over most of Africa, in association with permanent water. This species also occurs in Somalia, Ethiopia, the Democratic Republic of Congo and Angola.

Darting Cruiser

Phyllomacromia picta

Average size: ± 42 mm.

Description: The lower forehead of this dragonfly is yellow above, shading to red. The wing spot ranges from red to deep brown. The black and yellow abdomen is ± 32 mm long and the greenish thorax has yellow diagonal stripes. Hindwing length is ± 35 mm. The male's tenth abdominal segment bears a broad dorsal[G] cone (i.e. a cone-shaped portion jutting out from the anal appendage[G]), with one protruding spine. Upper anal appendages[G] tend to be yellow. Females are duller, and have a small pair of anal appendages[G]. The male has a pronounced swelling on segments 7, 8 and 9. This is thought to be for display purposes.

Habitat and habits: Occurs in bush country or on the fringe of forests located near a river. This alert species hawks[G] insects, and often settles on branches.

Distribution: A fairly common species, found from the Eastern Cape to KwaZulu-Natal, and northwards to Mozambique and Zimbabwe, across to northern Botswana and into Namibia. Also occurs in Kenya and in Chad.

Strong Skimmer

Orthetrum brachiale

Average size:
± 45 mm.

Description: The lower lip of this dragonfly species is either entirely or partly black. The cross veins^G just below the leading edge of the wing (see pages 6–7) are mostly yellow, while the synthorax^G has one or more white diagonal stripes edged with brown or black. The golden yellow wing spot is ± 3 mm long. Adult males are mostly a rich powder blue colour, while adult females are dull blue. Immature specimens of both sexes are cream with dark markings on the abdomen and have diagonal stripes on the synthorax^G as do the adults.

Habitat and habits: Occurs in savanna, bush or woodland. May be encountered at stagnant pools, however most often found near fast-flowing rivers or streams. A fast flier, often settling on a favourite perch.

Distribution: Fairly common, and found throughout eastern

South Africa, as well as north to Mozambique and Zimbabwe, and across northern Botswana into Namibia. Uncommon in the dry west and absent from heavy forests. Occurs over most of Africa.

White-lined Skimmer

Orthetrum caffrum

Average size:
± 45 mm.

Description: The thorax of the blue adult male bears two diagonal and two lateral[G] white stripes. The lower lip is yellowish as are the cross veins[G] below the leading edge of the wing (see pages 6–7). The abdomen is fairly long (± 30 mm), while the hindwing is longer at ± 34 mm in length. The yellow wing spot is less than 5 mm long. Females are duller in colour, and have thicker bodies than males, while immature specimens are cream with dark markings on the thorax and abdomen. They, too, often show the same white markings on the thorax.

Habitat and habits: Occurs near pools or streams in bush or grassland; uncommon in dry areas. As with other *Orthetrum* species, it settles often.

Distribution: A common dragonfly species, found throughout eastern South Africa, as well as north to Mozambique and Zimbabwe, and across northern Botswana to Namibia. Occurs as far north as Sudan and Ethiopia, and is found from Angola to equatorial West Africa.

Epualet Skimmer

Orthetrum chrysostigma

Average size: ± 45 mm.

Description: Very similar to the last two blue species. The lower lip is yellowish, and the syn-thorax^G bears one white diagonal stripe. At 30 mm in length, the abdomen is 2 mm shorter than the hindwing and the orange-yellow wing spot is ± 3 mm long. The adult female is duller and more robust than the male, while the immature specimens of both sexes are similar to the Strong Skimmer (*Orthetrum brachiale*) and the White-lined Skimmer (*O. caffrum*), but may appear a little more yellow.

Habitat and habits: Occurs in bush, savanna and woodlands, but is scarce in dry areas. Not found in dense forest, swamps or at high altitudes. This dragon-fly is tolerant of waters with diverse pH values, and may be encountered near streams, rivers and pools.

Distribution: This species is common throughout eastern South Africa, as well as north to Mozambique and Zimbabwe and across northern Botswana to Namibia. Originally described from the Canary Islands. It is found throughout Africa.

Long Skimmer

Orthetrum trinacria

Average size:
± 52 mm.

Description: Adults are large and have a dark blue-black colour. The abdomen is long (± 37 mm) and the hindwing is shorter (± 34 mm long). The lower forehead has black or grey markings. The cross veins^G below the leading edge of the wing are yellow and there is often amber colouring at the wing base (see pages 6–7). Adult females look similar to males, but immatures of both sexes are creamy, with dark markings on thorax and abdomen, as in most skimmers.

Habitat and habits: This species occurs in bush near large pools or rivers, often in arid regions. Behaves and moves like a member of the large and primitive Gomphid family, flying low and strongly, and settling often, but is extremely alert.

Distribution: This dragonfly is common throughout eastern South Africa, north to Mozambique and Zimbabwe, across northern Botswana and into Namibia. A few records have come from the dry areas to the west. Occurs in lightly wooded areas of Africa, the Mediterranean and Iraq.

Black-pointed Skimmer

Nesciothemis farinosa

Average size:
± 45 mm.

Description: Easily misidenti-
fied as an *Orthetrum* species –
in fact it was originally classi-
fied as such. A robust species
of dragonfly. The male has a
varying amount of powdery
blue colouring over most of
the thorax and abdomen. There
is a black tip towards the tenth
abdominal segment. The
lower lip and lower legs are
mainly black. Normally a
yellow dorsal stripe is present
on the thorax. Adult females
are duller in colour, and
immature specimens start off
dull cream.

Habitat and habits: Black-
pointed Skimmers favour open
country, streams, rivers, bush
or woodland areas. Uncommon
in dry areas and absent from
forests. Behaves much like an
Orthetrum, settling often on
a favourite perch.

Distribution: This species is
common from the Western Cape
eastwards throughout South
Africa, north to Mozambique
and Zimbabwe, and across
northern Botswana to Namibia.
Originally described from
Limpopo Province, South Africa.

Yellow-veined Widow

Palpopleura jucunda jucunda

Average size:
± 25 mm.

Description: A small, beautiful dragonfly. The upper forehead behind the eyes (called the occiput), the sides of the thorax and the legs are pale yellow, and the wings are broad, with discontinuous yellow or orange and dark brown panels. Males, females and immatures are similar in appearance, but males are often a little larger and have a powder blue abdomen when fully mature.

Habitat and habits: Occurs on reeds and sedges at pools or marshes, but not in forests. A slow-flying species that settles often on vegetation.

Distribution: This subpecies is fairly common in suitable habitat from the Western Cape eastwards through South Africa to Mozambique and Zimbabwe, and across northern Botswana into Namibia. Yellow-veined Widows also occur up to equatorial Africa and across to the Ivory Coast. A race is found in Ethiopia and Sudan.

Lucia Widow

Palpopleura lucia

Average size:
± 30 mm.

Description: Another particularly beautiful insect, having wings that are blackish on the leading edge (see pages 6–7). The male is a handsome dragonfly with a metallic blue-black lower forehead and varying amounts of black and blue on the thorax and abdomen, which can be completely blue in some cases. There are two recognized forms of this small species: the male of the form *Palpopleura portia* has less black colouring than *P. lucia*. Immature specimens and females are similar, but lack the blue coloration on the body and have varying amounts of yellow on the abdomen.

Habitat and habits: Occurs near grassy or reedy pools and slug-gish streams and marshes, as well as in open country, woodland and bush. Both forms may occur together, but the form *P. lucia* is more common in warmer areas. This is a slow-flying species that settles often on vegetation.

Distribution: Common from the Western Cape eastwards through South Africa to Mozambique and Zimbabwe, and across northern Botswana into Namibia. Found throughout Africa.

Pied-spot

Hemistigma albipuncta

Average size: ± 34 mm.

Description: A beautiful dragonfly, similar in appearance to the Jaunty Dropwing (see page 50). It can be very variable in marking and colours, but this species is easily recognized by its bi-coloured (black and yellow) wing spot. The leading edges of the wings are yellow (see pages 6–7). The female and immature male's thorax is yellow, with black diagonal stripes, while the top portion of the synthorax[G] is black above and has a central cream-yellow longitudinal strip. Males are similar, but the top portion of the lower thorax is blue. The abdomen is bluish and black in fully mature specimens of both sexes. The eyes of this species are red on the top half and yellowish below.

Habitat and habits: Found at reedy pools, streams, swampy areas and in surrounding bush, woodland and light forest. Settles on favourite perches and in large groups, often alongside the Jaunty Dropwing (*Trithemis stictica*).

Distribution: A common species, particularly in Mozambique and the Okavango Delta. Occurs from KwaZulu-Natal westwards into Botswana and Namibia, northwards to Kenya, and westwards to Senegal, where it was first discovered.

Black Percher

Diplacodes lefebvrii

Average size:
± 32 mm.

Description: This dragonfly varies greatly in size and markings. Mature males are black, often with a waxy, blue-coloured coating (called pruinescence) on the abdomen. The eyes are dark and the lower forehead has a purple-blue metallic sheen. Wings are clear, with a dark wing spot. Females and immature male specimens show some yellow markings on the thorax and abdomen, while the face is yellow with a broad black band on the lower forehead. The wing spot is brownish-yellow.

Habitat and habits: Occurs at pools and rivers as well as swamps, marshes, and temporary pans. May be found some distance away from water.

Distribution: Originally described from Egypt. This is a common species, occurring over most of the region, with the exception of the southwestern Cape. Also found over most of the African continent, southern Europe, and western Asia, as well as Mauritius, Madagascar, and the Seychelles.

Broad Scarlet

Crocothemis erythraea

Average size: ± 43 mm.

Description: Males are heavy-bodied, red dragonflies with clear wings. The yellow wing spot is over 3 mm long. The abdomen is particularly broad and has a maximun width of 3 mm. A small amount of amber is present on the base of the wings (see pages 6–7). Females are pinkish-brown in colour with a greenish stripe running along the thorax between the wings (called a dorsal^G stripe). Immature specimens are often a golden brown colour.

Habitat and habits: Occurs near reedy pools or marshes, particularly around bul-rushes and sage. This species is not found in forests. Often settles on stalks or grass and even on the ground, but is an alert species.

Distribution: This species is common and is found in most parts of Africa. It is encountered in suitable habitat from the Western Cape east through South Africa to Mozambique and Zimbabwe, and across northern Botswana and Namibia. It is also found in parts of Europe and Asia, where it overlaps with *Crocothemis servilia erythrea* (probably a sub-species). Originally described from Monrovia.

Small Scarlet

Crocothemis sanguinolenta

Average size:
± 35 mm.

Description: This dragonfly species is very similar in appearance to the Broad Scarlet (*Crocothemis erythraea*) and the two are easily confused. The only noticeable distinguishing feature in the field is the wing spot, which is normally (but not always) red. That of the previous species tends to be more yellow and longer than 3 mm. Otherwise, this is generally a smaller species with a narrower abdomen, normally under 3 mm at its broadest. Females are dull pink or yellow in colour and immature specimens are similar.

Habitat and habits: Found at pools, swamps, streams or rivers in open country, bush or savanna. Settles often on reeds or twigs.

Distribution: Common in suitable habitat from the Western Cape northwards throughout southern Africa and most of the African continent, except in heavily forested areas. This species also occurs in Madagascar.

Horned Rockdweller

Bradinopyga cornuta

Average size: ± 45 mm.

Description: A brown dragonfly with cream spots and markings on its robust thorax. Wings are mostly clear, with clouded tips and dark veins on the leading edges (see pages 6–7). The wing spot is dark brown, while the abdomen is narrow, with a serrated appearance. Sexes appear alike.

Habitat and habits: Found in rocky areas near rivers, or at temporary rock pools, where the nymphs[G] eat tadpoles. Occurs mainly on granite formations, often seeking shade behind boulders. Body markings and texture provide excellent camouflage against rock or concrete.

Distribution: Suitable habitat in lower-lying areas from KwaZulu-Natal north to Mozambique and Zimbabwe, and in the Zambezi valley westwards to northern Botswana and Namibia. Occurs as far north as Kenya.

Banded Groundling

Brachythemis leucostica

Average size: ± 35 mm (female: ± 32 mm).

Description: The abdomen and thorax of mature males are black and the wings normally have a black band and a golden wing spot. Females do not have the black bands on the wing. The lower forehead has a black band, and is often coated with a metallic sheen. The female's lower forehead has a continuous broad black band at the base. Females and immature specimens are dull yellow with black markings on the thorax, while the abdomen is divided by black bands that occur on each of the segments. Small black dots appear in pairs on either side of a black line that runs the length of the upper side of the abdomen. Both sexes of this dragonfly have a cigar-shaped abdomen. The hindwings are short and broad in both sexes.

Habitat and habits: Occurs near pools and lakes, in open country or woodland. A gregariousG, low-flying species that is associated with water. Often seen flying around the legs of people or animals for short distances, in the hope of catching small insects disturbed by movement. Does not occur in deserts.

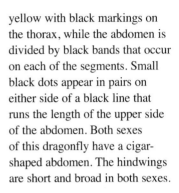

Distribution: Common in southern Africa, occurring in most open parts of the continent. Also found in Madagascar, southern Ethiopia and western Asia.

Red-veined Darter

Sympetrum fonscolombii

Average size:
± 38 mm.

Description: The synthorax[G] of this dragonfly is yellow to dull red, with white or greenish stripes on its sides. The abdomen of the adult male is deep pink or scarlet and the wings have red veins with a yellow wing spot. Superficially similar to the Red-veined Dropwing (see page 47), but lacks the patch of amber colouring at the base of the wings (see pages 6–7) and the dark wing spot. Females are less colourful than males.

Habitat and habits: Occurs near grassy or reedy pools in dry bush or arid surroundings. Thought to be migratory[G]. Behaves much like the Red-veined Dropwing (see page 47), and often settles on branches.

Distribution: This species is abundant in drier areas. Appears to be more common in southern Africa than north of the Zambezi River. Found from the Western Cape northwards through Botswana and Namibia, and eastwards through southern Zimbabwe into Mozambique. Occurs over many parts of the African continent, as well as in Madagascar, the Canary Islands, Madeira, Europe and Western Asia.

Barbet

Philonomon luminans

Average size:
± 38 mm.

Description: The abdomen of the male is red and yellow in equal parts. The thorax is often greenish with black markings. Eyes are reddish-brown above and grey-blue below, as in the Red-veined Dropwing (see page 47). The wings are generally clear, with a touch of amber at the base. The wing spot is golden brown. Females are similar, but are duller and more uniform in appearance, with less red in the markings.

Habitat and habits: This species occurs near reedy and grassy pools and sluggish streams at low altitudes, and in grassland or bush country. These dragonflies often settle on grass or on open ground.

Distribution: Absent from many parts of South Africa, but common from coastal KwaZulu-Natal northwards to Mozambique and Zimbabwe, and westwards to northern Botswana and into Namibia. This species has a range as far north as Somalia and across to Guinea. It has also been recorded on Assumption Island. The Barbet was originally described from Togo.

Violet Dropwing

Trithemis annulata

Average size:
± 40 mm.

Description: This dragonfly is a little larger than the Red-veined Dropwing (see page 47). The abdomen is broad – segments 4 and 5 are twice as long as they are broad. The lower forehead is a metallic violet colour, while the abdomen, and often the whole body, are purplish-red at maturity. The base of the wing has some amber colouring (see pages 6–7). Females are duller, brownish orange in colour, and have a very broad, pale cross band on abdominal segment 9, while segment 8 is black-edged and encloses a small amount of orange-brown.

Habitat and habits: Occurs near pools, lakes, streams and rivers, in woodland, bush, open country or arid semi-deserts. These dragonflies often settle on a favourite perch. Only absent from extremely dry areas.

Distribution: This species is common over most parts of southern Africa. Also found throughout Africa to the Mediterranean coast, as well as in southern Europe and western Asia.

Red-veined Dropwing

Trithemis arteriosa

Average size:
± 35 mm.

Description: Males are red and have medium-sized bodies. Abdominal segments 6 and 7 have a black band running along the sides of the segments. The wings have red veins and the wing spot is blackish-brown at maturity. Markings on the base of the wings are small, barely reaching the second antenodal[G] cross veins (see pages 6–7). Females have a duller, brownish to orange body. There is some black on the abdominal segments. Segment 9 is normally all black and the lower lip has a black band across the centre.

Habitat and habits: Like the Violet Dropwing (see page 46), this dragonfly occurs in lush, well-watered areas, as well as in arid conditions at small pools. Not found in extremely dry areas and in dense forest.

Distribution: A common species. Occurs in suitable habitat throughout southern Africa. Also encountered as far north as Somalia, and westward to Liberia, Morocco, the Canary Islands and western Asia.

Lakeside Dropwing

Trithemis dorsalis

Average size:
±38 mm.

Habitat and habits: Occurs at streams and pools in bush or open country, but not at higher altitudes, nor in forest.

Description: A dull bronze-brown to blue dragonfly. The synthorax^G has black lines that are not joined, while the abdomen is broad and tapering, and narrows slightly between the fourth and sixth segments. Adult males are covered in a powdery blue coating, which often obscures other markings. The lower forehead and eyes are dark, while the wings, which have black venation and a dark wing spot, are mostly clear, except for a small patch of amber at the base of the hindwing (see pages 6–7). Females are a dull brownish-red, with continuous black dorsal^G and lateral^G bands along the abdomen.

Distribution: Common from the Western Cape, across eastern and northern South Africa, eastern Botswana, Zimbabwe and Mozambique, as well as northwards to Kenya and the Democratic Republic of Congo.

Rock Dropwing

Trithemis kirbyi ardens

Average size:
± 36 mm.

Description: The male dragonfly has a red lower forehead and a bright crimson abdomen at maturity. The underside of the abdomen is light with a black longitudinal stripe. The lower (basal) halves of the wings are orange-yellow (see pages 6–7). The wing spot is very small. Females are brownish. Abdominal segments 8 and 9 have two pale lateralᴳ stripes or are pale with two black stripes. The female's hindwing has either an isolated yellow spot in the lower back (anal) region, or has pronounced yellow streaks near the base (see pages 6–7). Collectors should be careful not to confuse males of this species with the similar male of the Red Groundling (*Brachythemis lacustris*), which occurs sparsely in the northeast of the region.

Habitat and habits: Occurs near rivers or pools, settling on rocks, stones or sandy banks. Common in arid country, but is not found in forest. The female often stays secluded among bushes.

Distribution: *T. k. ardens* is found throughout South Africa and all countries in the region, except in the Namib, as little or no standing water occurs here. Occurs north to Ethiopia, west to Senegal and also in Madagascar and the Comores. *T. kirbyi* occurs in Asia.

Jaunty Dropwing

Trithemis stictica

Average size:
± 34 mm.

Description: This is a fairly slender species of dragonfly. The wings are normally clear, although the hindwing may have a slight yellowish tint. The wing spot is light brown. The male's lower forehead is steely blue above, while the thorax is bright yellow and pale blue with some black stripes. The top of the female's forehead is broadly black with a strong blue-green sheen and the yellow thorax has lateral^G lines linked by an irregular band. The fourth and seventh abdominal segments are yellow, with a streak on each side, while the fourth and fifth are about twice as long as they are broad.

Habitat and habits: Occurs in bush, forest and litus^G, reedy streams, pools or swamps, settling often on reeds or branches. Like the Red-veined Dropwing (see page 47), adults are found almost throughout the year.

Distribution: This species is common from coastal KwaZulu-Natal to the Limpopo Province, eastern and northern Botswana, Caprivi, Zimbabwe and Mozambique. Also found in Ethiopia, the Ivory Coast and Madagascar.

Ringed Cascader

Zygonyx torridus

Average Size:
± 50 mm.

Description: This large, robust dragonfly is easily recognizable in flight. The wings are long and broad (longer than the abdomen), with a black wing spot. There is a slight yellow tinge to the wings, which are strengthened by a structure of thick black veins, and there is a white supporting structure or membranule at the base of each hindwing (see pages 6–7). The thorax is generally black with broken yellow diagonal stripes or spots. The abdomen is spotted yellow (against black) on the sides and top of all but the tenth segment. Eyes and lower forehead are dark (metallic violet in males) in colour, while the upper lip is sometimes yellow. Sexes are similar.

Habitat and habits: This species is solitary and occurs only at river rapids or waterfalls, where it breeds. It hovers intermittently while hunting over water.

Distribution: This species is fairly common and occurs over most of southern Africa, with the exception of the southwestern part of the Western Cape. Found throughout nearly all of Africa. There are races (subspecies) in Mauritius, southern India, southern Europe and western Asia. Originally described from Sierra Leone.

Phantom Flutterer

Rhyothemis semihyalina

Average size: ± 32 mm.

Description: A particularly beautiful medium-sized dragonfly in which sexes are similar, both in size and appearance. The thorax and abdomen are black. The forewings are generally clear, with a yellowish tinge. The hindwing in adults has a distinctive metallic brownish-black or purplish panel. The wing spot is black.

Habitat and habits: The Phantom Flutterer occurs near reedy pools and lakes in open or bush country. Not found in dense forest. A solitary species that has a slow, butterfly-like flight.

Distribution: Common in most of Africa. Occurs from southeastern South Africa to Mozambique and Zimbabwe, and westwards across central and northern Botswana to northern Namibia.

Wandering Glider

Pantala flavescens

Average size: ± 48 mm.

Description: This dragonfly's orange abdomen has variable black markings, a white stripe along the base, and is ± 40 mm long. The robust, greenish thorax is shiny and almost wrinkled in appearance. It is also quite hairy in places. The wings are clear, often with a white border to the supporting structure at the base, which is called the membranule (see pages 6–7). The golden yellow wing spot measures ± 3 mm. Sexes are similar, however adult males are a deeper orange on the abdomen.

Habitat and habits: Occurs in almost any habitat. The females frequently lay their eggs in small temporary pools and the larvae[G] develop rapidly. This gregarious[G] species may be seen flying in large numbers ahead of a storm and can often be found scouring lawns for insects during the summer months.

Distribution: A very common migrant[G] found throughout southern Africa, with the exception of the Namib Desert. Found throughout Africa and tropical[G], subtropical[G], and temperate[G] regions around the world. Originally described from India.

Wheeling Glider

Tramea basilaris

Average size:
± 48 mm.

Description: An easily recognizable dragonfly, this species has an orange-brown body. The wing spot is yellow, while the lower region of the hindwing (the basal area, see pages 6–7) has orange-yellow panels surrounding dark brown bars or spots. The sexes are similar.

Habitat and habits: This migratory^G species is found near quiet waters, slow rivers and pools and often in, or near, woodland. It tends to settle now and then on twigs and reeds, but is alert and fast flying.

Distribution: This is a fairly common species that is found from the Eastern Cape northwards to Mozambique, northern South Africa and Zimbabwe, and westwards into northern Botswana and Namibia. Occurs over most of Africa. It is also found on remote Assumption Island and in Asia.

Blue Basker

Urothemis edwardsii

Average size:
± 40 mm.

Description: The abdomen of this dragonfly is covered by a broad black dorsal^G band. Males have a dark blue, powdery coating. The hindwing has a small, mainly black panel at the base, with some radiating amber, while the wing spot is golden yellow and 3 mm or more in length (see pages 6–7). The female is similar to the male.

Habitat and habits: This species prefers large bodies of quiet water but is also common in and around swamplands.
It tends to settle persistently on the same reeds, even if chased away repeatedly.

Distribution: This fairly common species is found from coastal KwaZulu-Natal northwards to Mozambique, northern South Africa and Zimbabwe, and westwards across eastern and northern Botswana and Namibia. Also occurs northwards to Sudan and westwards to Guinea, and has been recorded from Algeria.

Glossary

Anal appendages: Appendages on the tenth abdominal segment. The male's upper (superior) and lower (inferior) pair are used to clasp the female during copulation.

Antenodal: Before the *nodus,* an indentation along the leading edge of the wing that acts as a strengthening feature.

Cross veins: Intersecting veins in the wing (see pages 6–7)

Cerci: See stylets.

Diurnal: Active during the day.

Dorsal (dorsally): Referring to the back.

Entomologist: A person who studies insects.

Gregarious: Living together in colonies or groups.

Hawk(ing): Hunting or searching for prey in the manner of a hawk (flying slowly, scanning the area).

Larva(e): See nymph.

Lateral: Of, or relating to, the side or sides.

Litus: Extensive lakes, swamps, rivers and thickly forested streams.

Migrant (migratory): Journeying between different habitats at specific times of the year.

Naphthalene: White crystalline substance used as an insect repellant (mothballs).

Nocturnal: Active at night.

Nymph: A pre-adult form that undergoes metamorphosis.

Posterior: At the back or rear.

Prehensile: Capable of curling round and grasping objects.

Stylets/cerci: Small, protruding appendages on the tenth abdominal segment in female dragonflies.

Subtropical: The region lying between the tropics and temperate lands.

Synthorax: Large section of the thorax that supports the wings. It is divided into four segments.

Temperate: A climate that is never extremely hot or extremely cold.

Terrestrial: Living on land.

Tropical: The part of the Earth's surface between the tropics of Cancer and Capricorn.

Ventral: Of or on the abdomen.

Further Reading

Tarboton, W & Tarboton, M. 2002. *A Fieldguide to the Dragonflies of South Africa.* Johannesburg: Privately published.